Elementary Level

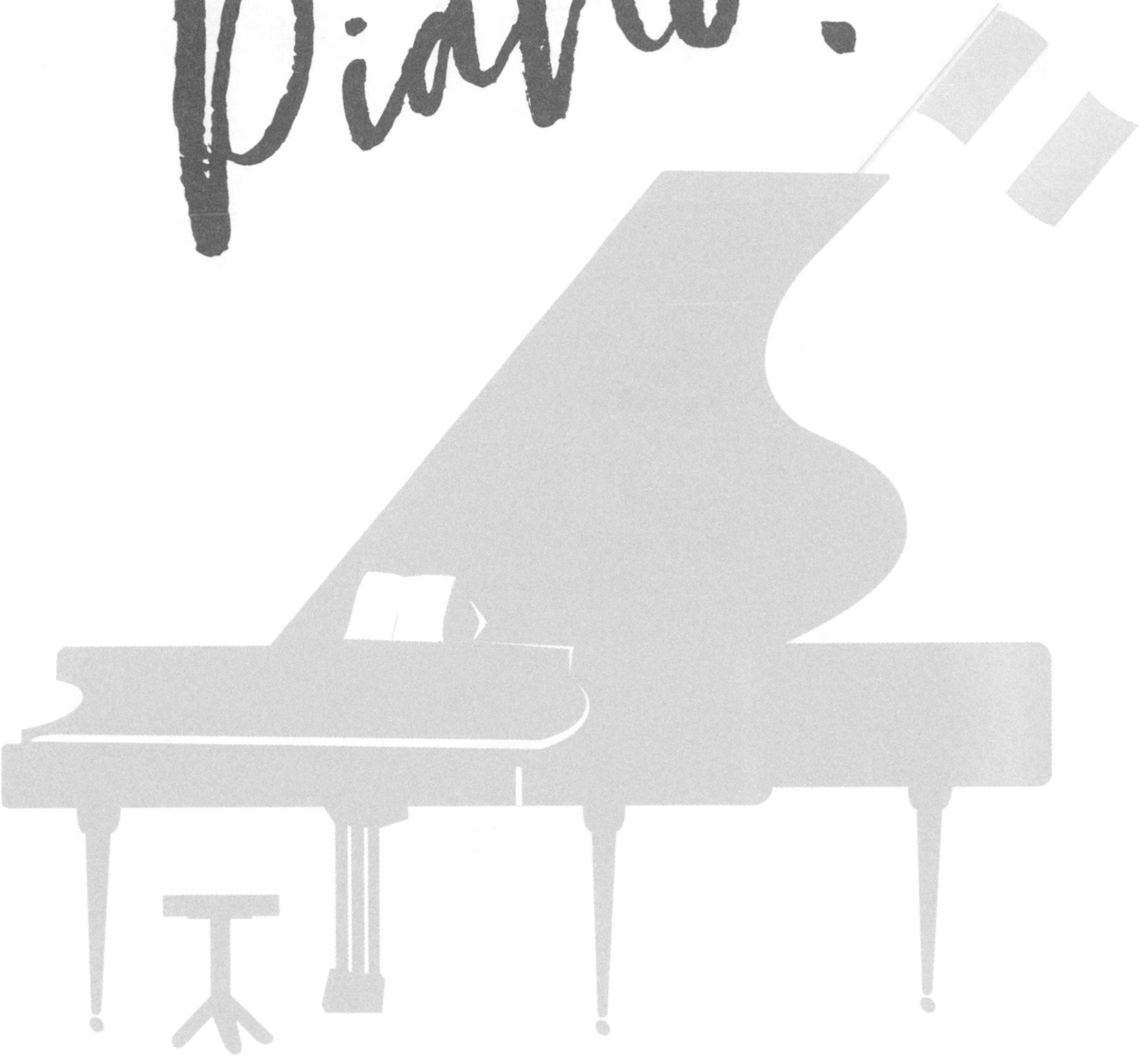

Bonjour, Piano!

ISBN 978-1-4950-8865-0

Visit Hal Leonard Online at
www.halleonard.com

CONTENTS

Editorial suggestions in the music appear in brackets.

COMPOSER BIOGRAPHIES

JEAN-MICHEL ARNAUD
(b. 1928)

Jean-Michel Arnaud was born in Paris. In his earliest piano training he was frustrated with a teacher who stifled creativity and improvisation. At age 12 he encountered more open-minded teachers at the Conservatoire. At 17 he began to teach in an unorthodox way, writing short pieces for his students and allowing them to choose the titles. This method was later crystallized in his piano method books *Le Piano Ouvert*, *Le Piano Decouvert*, and others. Arnaud wrote lyrics for the pieces in *Le Piano Ouvert*, and the book includes recordings of himself and children singing along. He has taught piano in several schools in the Paris area, and has been invited to open "pilot" classes as alternatives to traditional music teaching. In addition to teaching, Arnaud has composed a string quartet, a quartet for string trio and flute, and a choral piece titled *La mu-si-que*.

MÉLANIE "MEL" BONIS
(1858-1937)

Mélanie Bonis was born into a Parisian lower middle-class family of strong Catholic morals. Despite the child showing early signs of musical talent, her parents only agreed to let her study music after a recommendation from a friend who was professor of cornet at the Conservatoire. At age 16, she met César Franck, who gave her piano lessons. In a singing class, she developed a close relationship with Amédée Landély Hettich, a singing student and poet, and began setting his poems to music. Mélanie's parents strongly disapproved of her romance with Hettich. They forced her out of the Conservatoire and arranged a marriage for her in 1883 to Albert Domange, a businessman with no real affinity for music. Eventually Mélanie began meeting with Hettich again as an outlet for new composition and returning to the music scene. Their reunion eventually led to an illegitimate child, who she had to hide for much of her life. In the following years she put all her energy into her music and became a member of the SCM (Société des compositeurs de musique). She received performances of her music by some of the finest musicians of the time, and composed about three hundred works in all, though few were published. She used the name "Mel" because women composers were viewed disparagingly in her era.

OLIVIER HAURAY
(b. 1952)

Olivier Hauray was trained in organ and piano at the Caen Conservatory and with private teachers, and studied musicology at the Sorbonne. His career has been dedicated entirely to teaching piano; *Introduction to the piano by styles* volumes 1 and 2 are the result of his experiences as pedagogue confronted with the difficulties that student pianists have to solve. The books contain Hauray's original pedagogical pieces, emulating musical styles from Baroque to jazz, and proposing the technical solutions for their expressive purpose. Olivier Hauray continues to compose according to his musical encounters and his educational projects.

ERIK SATIE
(1866-1925)

One of the most eccentric personalities in all of music, Satie began piano studies in 1874, with a teacher who instilled a love of medieval music and chant. He entered the Paris Conservatoire in 1878, and was expelled two and a half years later for lack of talent. He was readmitted in 1885, but did not change the minds of his professors. After a detour in the Infantry – seen for a moment as a better career choice – Satie settled in the artistic Paris neighborhood of Montmartre in 1887. There he composed his first pieces: *Ogives*, for piano, written without barlines (a compositional choice found frequently in Satie's music) and the famous *Gymnopédies*. In 1890, while pianist and conductor at the cabaret Le Chat Noir, he met Claude Debussy and joined the spiritual movement Rose-Croix du Sâr Péladan (Rosicrucian Order), eventually becoming a choirmaster for the group. His involvement inspired the works *Sonneries de la Rose+Croix* and *Le Fils des Etoiles*. He had a brief and passionate relationship with the painter Suzanne Valadon in 1893. Brokenhearted after Suzanne left, he wrote *Vexations*, a theme to be played 840 times in a row – about twenty hours. In 1895 Satie abandoned his usual red robe and replaced it with seven identical mustard velvet suits, nicknaming himself "the Velvet Gentleman." In the next few years he moved to the suburb of Arcueil, and began taking composition lessons at the Schola Cantorum. He met Jean Cocteau, with whom he collaborated on the ballet *Parade* in 1916. Satie gradually met more artists of the French avant-garde, and presided over the birth of the group "Les Six." He died in 1925 of cirrhosis of the liver – probably due to his abundant consumption of absinthe. His friends visited his room in Arcueil – to which he had denied access throughout his life – and they discovered the state of poverty in which Satie had always lived.

ALEXANDRE TANSMAN
(1897-1986)

Tansman was born in Łódź, Poland, but lived in France for most of his life. While in Poland he trained in music at the Łódź Conservatory and completed a doctorate in law at the University of Warsaw (1918). After moving to Paris in 1920, he met Stravinsky and Ravel, both of whom encouraged his work. Tansman found his way into the École de Paris, a group of foreign musicians that included Bohuslav Martinů. Tansman enjoyed international success, with his orchestral music performed under such esteemed conductors as Koussevitzky, Toscanini, and Stokowski. During an American concert tour as pianist with Koussevitzky and the Boston Symphony in 1927, Tansman met George Gershwin. His concertizing also took him to Europe, Asia, Palestine and India, where he was a guest of Mahatma Gandhi in 1933. He gained French citizenship in 1938, but because of his Jewish heritage, he and his family were soon forced to flee France to the United States. Settled in Los Angeles, Tansman became acquainted with Schoenberg and composed a number of film scores. He returned to Paris in 1946. His honors included the Coolidge Medal (1941), election to the Académie Royale of Belgium (1977) and the Polish Medal of Cultural Merit (1983). He composed hundreds of pieces in total, exploring practically every musical genre, from symphonies to ballets to chamber music and works for solo guitar.

POINTS FOR PRACTICE AND TEACHING

In Brittany / *En Bretagne*
Jean-Michel Arnaud

- Brittany (Bretagne) is a region on the northwest coast of France.
- Note that the five-finger position for both hands stays the same throughout the piece. All the notes are right under your fingers.
- Try to create a smooth transition from R.H. to L.H. in m. 2.
- Notice the contrary motion in m. 5-6 and 9-10; the R.H. descends while the L.H. ascends.
- Make sure to play ***p*** in m. 8, like an echo of the previous phrase.
- In m. 9, the dynamic returns to ***mf***.

From the Orient / *Orientale*
from I Play for Mama / *Je joue pour maman*
Alexandre Tansman

- This is an excellent piece for students learning to play hands together.
- The hands have a different five-finger position than the last piece, but once again they stay in that position for the whole piece.
- The L.H. plays the same 2-note chord for the first 16 measures! This is what we a call a drone—a bass note or chord that holds or repeats under a melody.
- The L.H. drone is meant to represent an exotic instrument like the Indian *tambura*.
- Play the R.H. louder than the left-hand drone throughout.
- Be aware of sudden dynamic changes; ***p*** in m. 1-8, ***f*** in m. 9-12, etc.
- In m. 17-24, when the bass becomes more active, aim for a rhythmic, dancelike quality.

Gypsy Air / *Air Bohémien*
from I Play for Mama / *Je joue pour maman*
Alexandre Tansman

- Tansman is teaching cut-time, where the half note is the beat instead of the usual quarter note.
- This piece might sound similar sound to the previous one, but the shifting hand positions and moving L.H. line make this more complex.
- Once you've learned m. 1-16, you've learned two-thirds of the piece! M. 1-16 and m. 33-48 are exactly the same.
- In m. 2-3 and 10-11, the change from 4th finger on C to 5th finger on E might be a stretch for smaller hands. Practice the change with a smooth rocking motion in the wrist, letting the hand rotate toward the next note to make the stretch easier.
- Play the L.H. alone in m. 17-24, then in m. 25-31. Listen to the difference between the tied notes and the whole notes that are played once per measure, as well as the ending of the second phrase.
- Also note that the sequences in m. 17-24 and 25-31 both involve downward motion by step. The hand never has to leave the starting position.
- We have added dynamics to the piece for more character.

Game of Hands / *Jeux de Mains*
Olivier Hauray

- This piece is indeed a bit of a game: a study in hand crossing. The challenge is to maintain a smooth, continuous melody even while changing hands, and to keep the hands from bumping into each other as they cross!
- Note the key signature of D Major. All F's and C's are sharp.
- Try playing just the first note of each measure, but with the correct hand and finger, to get a preview of how the hands will move.
- During this exercise, practice sliding the hand playing toward you, away from the keyboard, as you switch to the other hand.
- It makes the most sense for the hands to cross *over* one another, except in m. 9 where the L.H. crosses under.

Arabian Melody / *Mélodie Arabe*
from I Play for Mama / *Je joue pour maman*
Alexandre Tansman

- Both hands stay in their initial five-finger position through the whole piece.
- The drone in the L.H. continues through the whole piece.
- Note that the fourth finger in the R.H. plays D-sharp instead of D natural.
- The D-sharp makes the music sound like an exotic scale from the Middle East.
- Try playing a five-note scale from A to E on all white keys, then try it while plaing D-sharp instead of D and note the difference.

Waltz / *Valse*
from I Play for Mama / *Je joue pour maman*
Alexandre Tansman

- This simple but sweet waltz should flow steadily.
- Practice hands separately.
- This piece contains three sections: m. 1-24, m. 25-40, and m. 41 to the end.
- Note the changes in the L.H. pattern. It might help to make a mark in the music at the points where the pattern changes.
- You could also master the L.H. part by practicing m. 1-24 as chords, with all three notes played at the same time, to feel the change in hand position.
- Note that in m. 13-14, the R.H. second finger jumps onto the E right after the third finger. Master this transition by practicing m. 13-14 several times.

Little Problem / *Petit Problème*
from I Play for Papa / *Je joue pour papa*
Alexandre Tansman

- Notice that Tansman has marked the half note as the beat, even though the time signature is 4/4.
- Here Tansman is introducing the student to Baroque style, in which the two hands are fairly independent. Practice the hands separately.
- Note the R.H. stretch in m. 7 from 1 on B to 2 on E.
- In m. 9 the R.H. thumb crosses under the fourth finger.
- Prepare for the leap in m. 16-17. Don't be afraid to take a slight pause at the end of the phrase in m. 16 to allow yourself time.
- The piece is in two distinct sections: m. 1-16 and m. 17-32.
- M. 17-24 contain what is called a sequence: a musical motive restated at a different pitch in the same voice. The two phrases of the sequence are m. 17-20 and m. 21-24.

The Princess of Tulips / *Ce qui dit la Princesse des Tulipes*
from Childish Small Talk / *Menus Propos enfantins*
Erik Satie

- Both hands are in five-finger position: R.H. thumb on D above middle C, L.H. thumb on C above middle C.
- With only white notes, this piece may look easy, but it has some unpredictable turns.
- Each phrase should be played as if sung on a smooth breath, *legato* and with no accents.
- The R.H. and the L.H. have different lengths of phrases, beginning and ending at different points.
- Notice the rests in the R.H. on beats 3-4 of m. 4, 8, and 16. Make sure not to hold the R.H. note too long in these spots.
- Read Satie's text to yourself, but do not read it aloud while playing! The composer forbade it.

Fishing / *À la pêche*
Jean-Michel Arnaud

- Note the tempo heading: Flowing. The music should flow easily.
- Begin practice with hands separate.
- From measure 4 into measure 5, the R.H. jumps from fourth finger to third finger on the same F. It may seem odd, but these changes in fingering help you to get set for future notes that would otherwise be out of reach.
- From measure 6 to measure 7, another finger switch happens as the R.H. jumps from fourth finger to fifth finger on G.
- In m. 11-14, the R.H. starts the third finger on four different notes at the beginnings of phrases. Make sure to lift a bit at the end of each phrase in m. 11-13 to move to the new position.
- Notice how for most of the piece, the R.H. has longer phrases than the L.H..
- Note dynamic contrasts and the *crescendos* and *decrescendos* in m. 5-6, m. 9-10, and m. 11-13.

The Mouse / *Souris*
Jean-Michel Arnaud

- The R.H. stays in five-finger position throughout, with the thumb on middle C.
- The L.H. plays thirds throughout. Start by practicing the L.H. alone.
- The movement between thirds requires practice and patience, and some fingering may need to be altered.
- Note the marking of *legato*; everything should be played smoothly. Try to create the *legato* with your fingers, without the use of pedal.
- In m. 41, the L.H. has the fastest-moving thirds in the piece, but it happens during a tempo *rallentando*, so you can ease into the changes.

In Three / *À trois temps*
from I Play for Papa / *Je joue pour papa*
Alexandre Tansman

- The title "In Three" refers to the time signature of 3/4.
- At the tempo of ♩=126, each beat of the measure is felt, rather than at faster tempos where ¾ might be felt "in one," with each measure acting as a beat.
- This piece contains a variety of fingering challenges.
- From m. 9 into m. 10, the R.H. thumb has to cross under the fourth finger. Practice this swinging motion at a slow tempo.
- From m. 12 into m. 13, the R.H. second finger has to cross over the thumb. This requires less movement than the previous cross, but it should still be practiced slowly.
- The last cross is from m. 18 to 19, where the L.H. thumb crosses under the third finger.
- In m. 18, note that the R.H. jumps from 4 to 3 on C.
- Play the L.H. in m. 2-6 alone and hear the descending line.
- The L.H. part becomes more active in m. 12 to the end. Tansman is using two independent voices to create a complex texture that we call *counterpoint*.

Madrigal / *Madrigal*
from Album for the Very Young, Op. 103 / *Album pour les tout-petits, Op. 103*
Mélanie Bonis

- The composer has written specific articulations for the L.H.: two-note phrases with the second note played *staccato*. The R.H.'s phrases vary in length, but are usually longer than the L.H. It is important to follow this phrasing to keep the *grazioso* (graceful) quality of the music.
- Make sure to lean into the first note of all the R.H. two-note phrases.
- Lift up short from the *staccato* second notes of left-hand phrases.
- The tiny note in m. 14 is a *grace note*. The slash through the note means that it is played slightly before the beat.
- The R.H. has a large reach from m. 30 to m. 31—a full octave from G to G. Practice a smooth wrist rotation toward the top note to help with the stretch.
- This piece contains several musical sequences. Listen to the similarity between m. 1-4 and m. 5-8, and also between m. 17-19 and m. 20-23.
- A surprising turn occurs in m. 23: the ending note of the phrase becomes the first note of a repeat of the opening section.

On the Hunt / *À la chasse*

Jean-Michel Arnaud

- In earlier centuries, horns of various kinds were played as hunting calls. They could only play a few pitches, but had a distinctive sound. This piece imitates the sound of those horns.
- Both hands stay in five-finger position, with the R.H. thumb on middle C and the L.H. thumb on B below middle C.
- The L.H. only plays two different notes throughout the piece.
- Practice the changing thirds in m. 5-6, 13-14, 17, and 19 slowly.
- In m. 17-20, a phrase marked ***f*** is followed by the same phrase marked ***p***. Think of this as the distant echo of the hunting horn.
- Note that after playing through the piece, it repeats from the beginning before ending in m. 16 at the **Fine** (the Italian word for "end").

Blue Note / *Note "bluesée"*

Olivier Hauray

- In blues and jazz music, certain pitches in the scale are flattened. The "blue notes" in this piece are E-flat and A-flat.
- The L.H. pattern is a simplified version of what you might play in a standard blues tune.
- Note the rests in between L.H. notes; don't hold the quarter notes too long.
- From m. 4 to m. 5, and then from m. 8 to m. 9, both hands move to new positions. Practice this transition slowly. The apostrophe (') marks at the end of of m. 4 and m. 8 mean that you can take a tiny pause before the next measure.
- Blues music is very important to the development of popular music in the United States, and blues and jazz have also influenced many French composers.

The Injured Bird / *L'Oiseau blessé*

Jean-Michel Arnaud

- Both hands are in five-finger position: R.H. thumb on D above middle C and L.H. thumb on middle C.
- The music sounds surprisingly complex for five-finger position. Skilled composers know how to work well with limitations.
- In m. 13-16, the two hands move in parallel motion. Practice this section slowly, making sure the hands move together as one.
- Note the dynamic contrasts. The piece begins ***mp***, then changes to ***f*** in m. 9, and down to ***p*** in m. 12. M. 13-14 are ***f***, with a *decrescendo* in m. 15 and another in m. 18.
- Practice hands separately to hear the difference in phrase lengths.

The Fortune Teller / *La bonne aventure*

Jean-Michel Arnaud

- Note the mixture of long and short phrases. M. 1-4 and m. 9-12 contain four-bar phrases, and then m. 5-8 are made up of 2-bar phrases. M. 13-20 are a mixture of two-bar and one-bar phrases.
- Because of tricky fingering changes, practice hands separately.
- In m. 2, the second finger of the R.H. crosses over the thumb and back, and the L.H. thumb crosses under the second finger.
- In m. 4, the L.H. third finger jumps from 1 to 3 on G.
- M. 5-6 and m. 7-8 contain a two-part musical sequence.
- At the end of the piece, the marking **D.C. al Fine** means to play from the beginning again, including the repeat, until the **Fine** in m. 12.
- Note the dynamic changes: ***f*** beginning in m. 1, ***mf*** in m. 13, and ***p*** in m. 17. Also observe the *crescendos* and *decrescendos* in m. 6-8 and m. 19-20.

– Brendan Fox
editor

This page has been left blank to avoid unnecessary page turns.

In Brittany

Jean-Michel Arnaud

From the Orient

from *I Play for Mama*

Alexandre Tansman

Moderately [𝅗𝅥 = 80]

5

9

13

17

21
p

25
2 3 4 2
3
f

29
5
1 2 3 4
p

33
5
f

37
4 3 2
1
p

Gypsy Air

from *I Play for Mama*

Alexandre Tansman

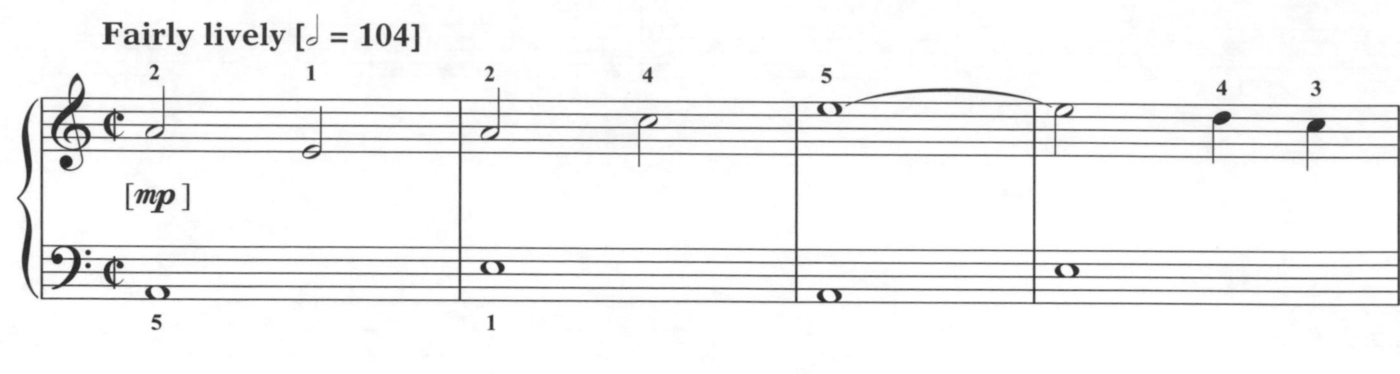

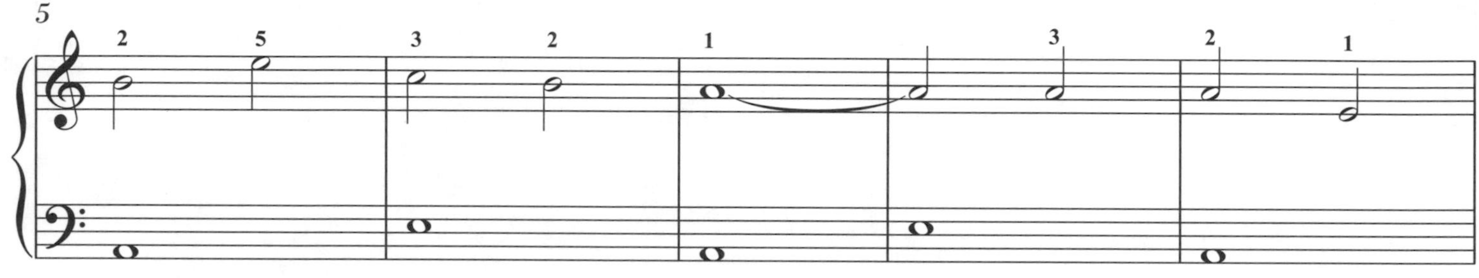

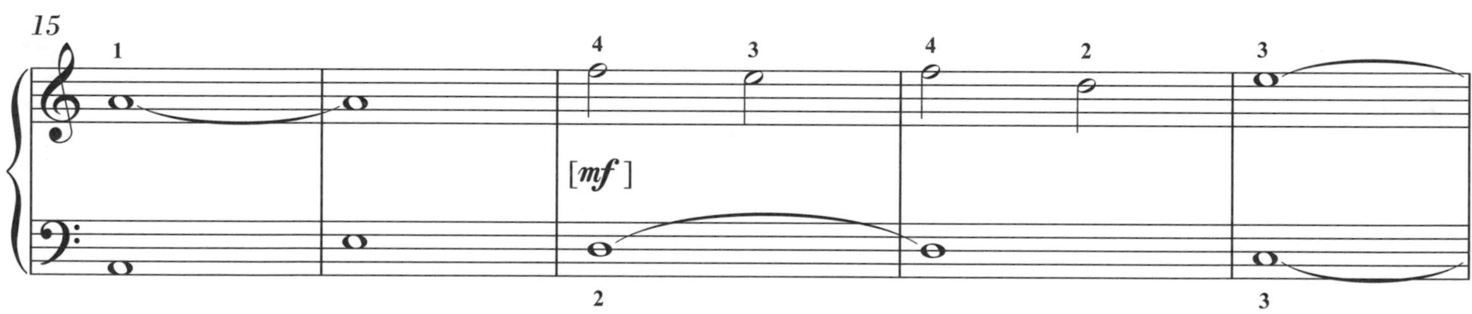

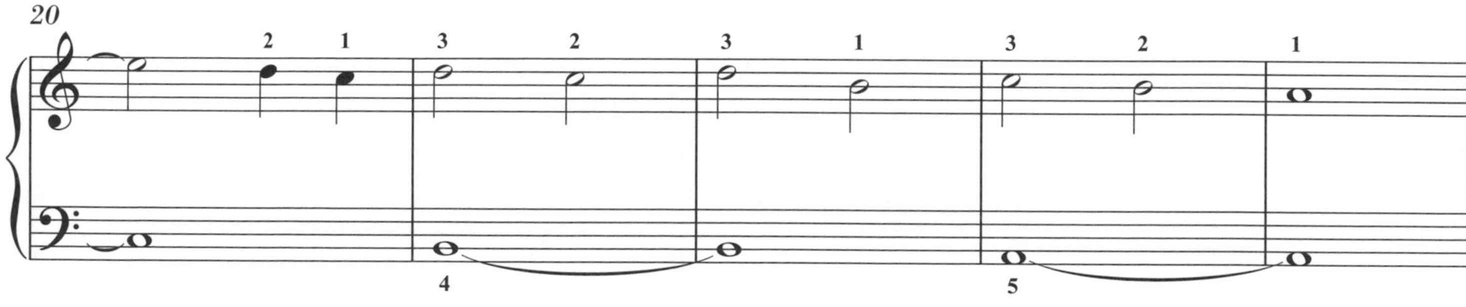

25
4
3
4
2
3
2
3
1
4
2
2
3
4

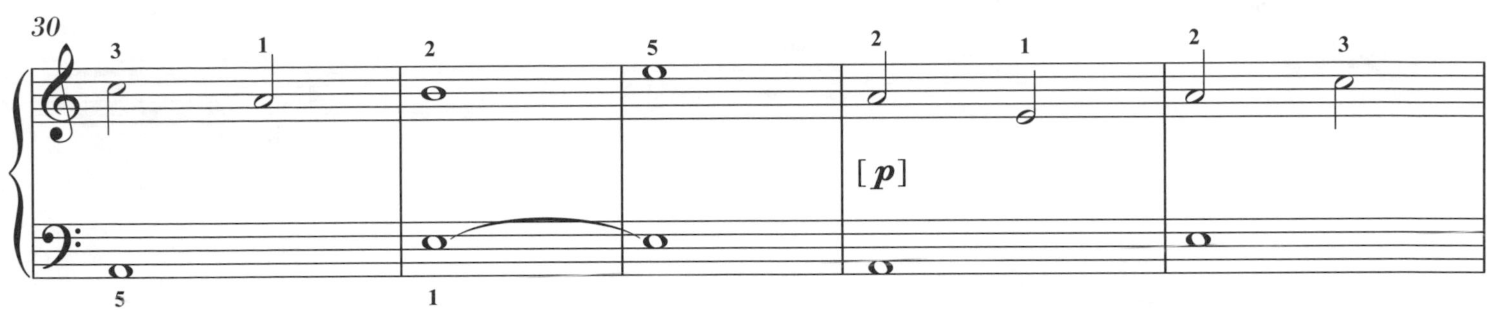
30
3
1
2
5
2
1
2
3
[p]
5
1

35
5
4
3
2
5
3
2

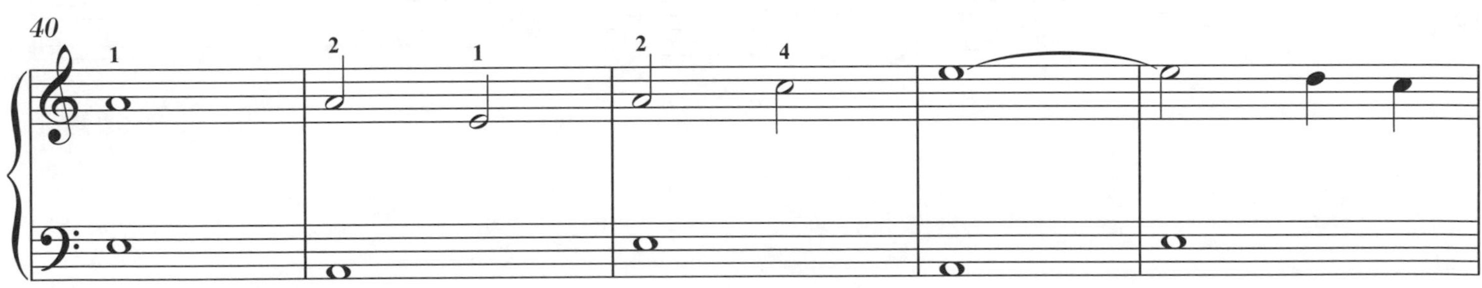
40
1
2
1
2
4

45

Game of Hands

Olivier Hauray

Arabian Melody

from *I Play for Mama*

Alexandre Tansman

Waltz

from *I Play for Mama*

Alexandre Tansman

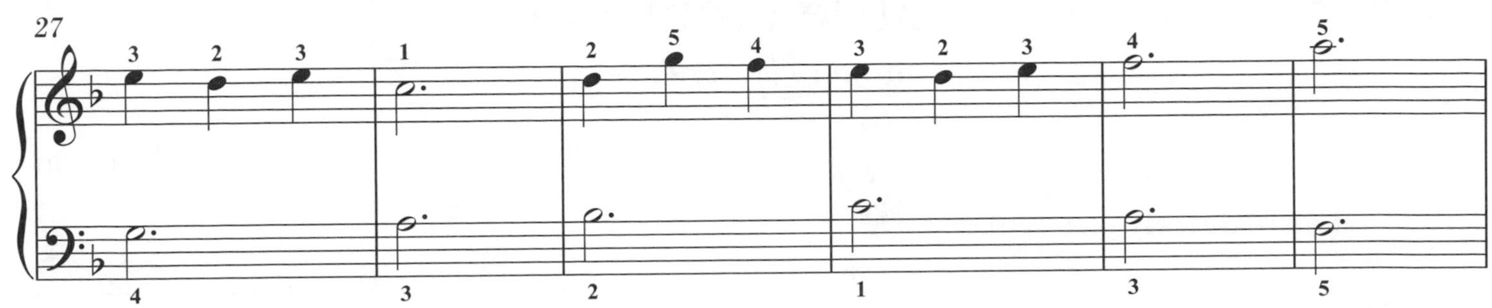
27
3
2
3
1
2
5
4
3
2
3
4
5
4
3
2
1
3
5

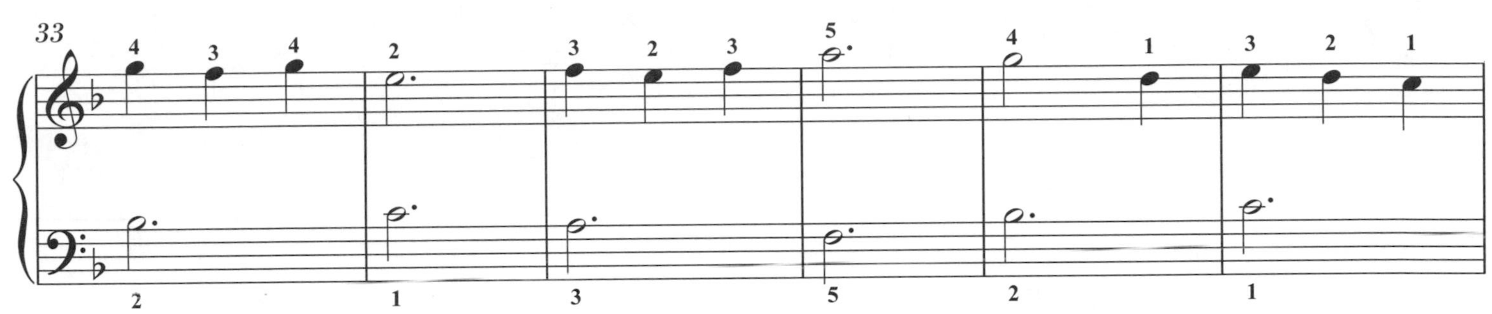
33
4
3
4
2
3
2
3
5
4
1
3
2
1
2
1
3
5
2
1

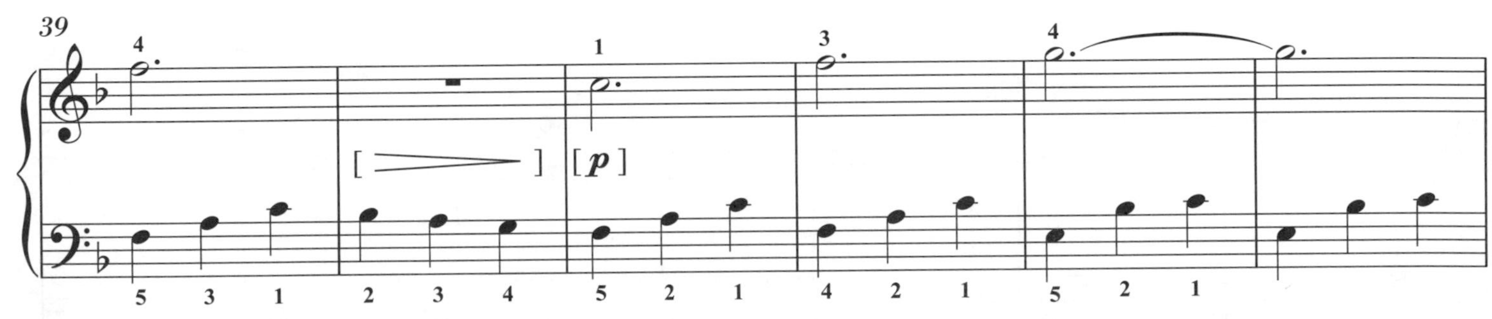
39
4
1
3
4
[p]
5
3
1
2
3
4
5
2
1
4
2
1
5
2
1

45
4
5

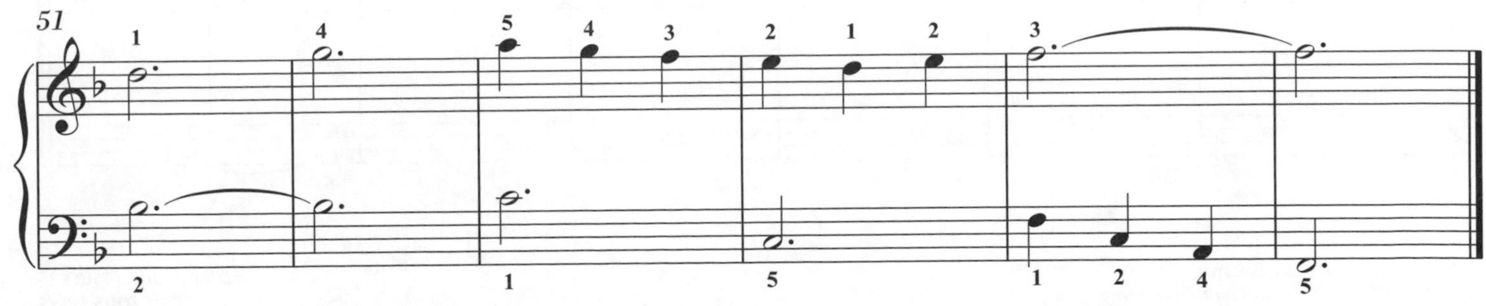
51
1
4
5
4
3
2
1
2
3
2
1
5
1
2
4
5

Little Problem

from *I Play for Papa*

Alexandre Tansman

The Princess of Tulips

from *Childish Small Talk*

Erik Satie

Satie often included phrases of narrative text in his piano music. He forbade these to be read aloud during performance.

Fishing

Jean-Michel Arnaud

[Flowing ♩ = 124]

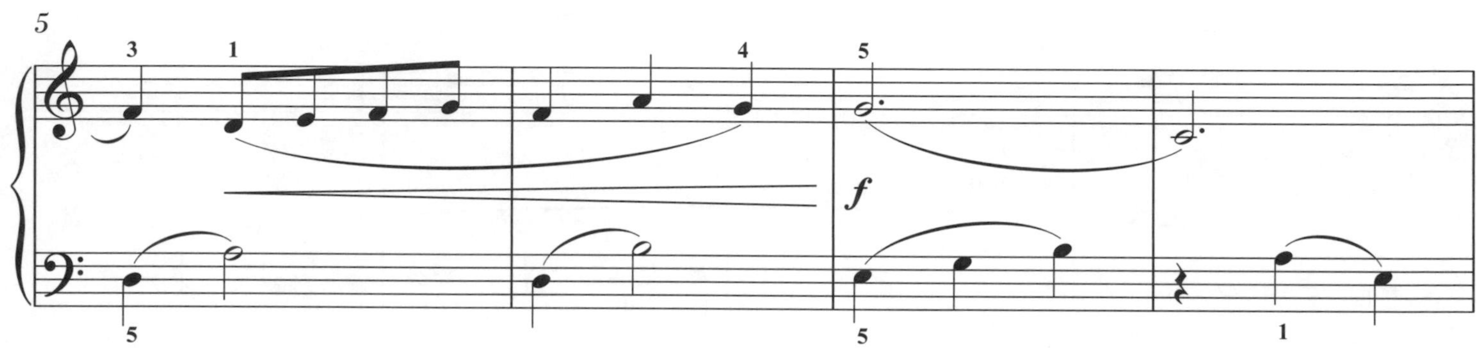

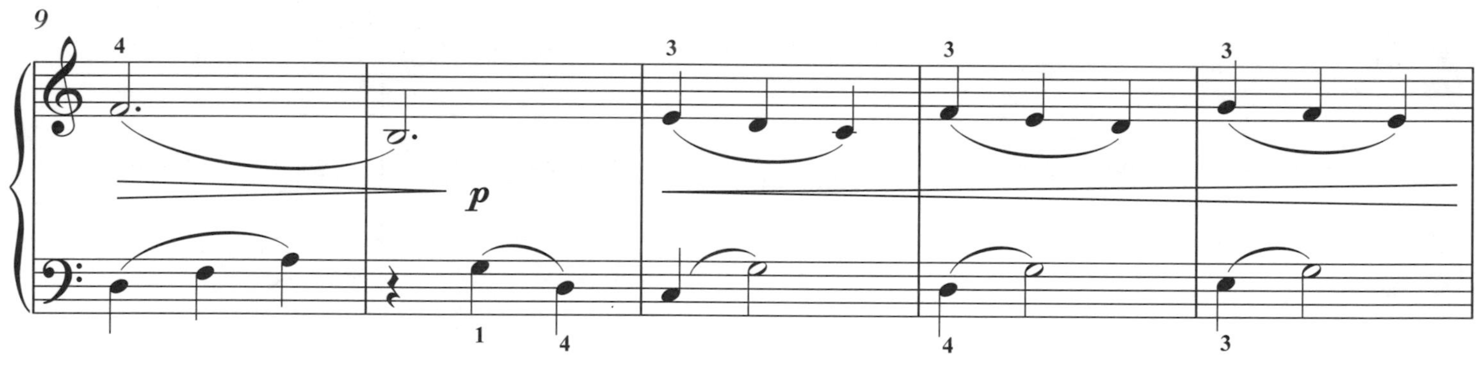

The Mouse

Jean-Michel Arnaud

This page has been left blank to avoid unnecessary page turns.

In Three

from *I Play for Papa*

Alexandre Tansman

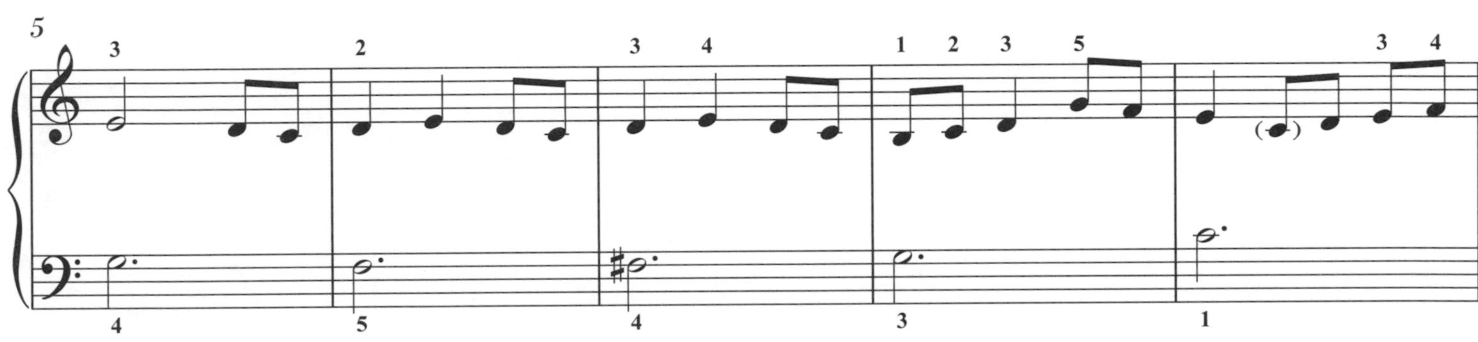

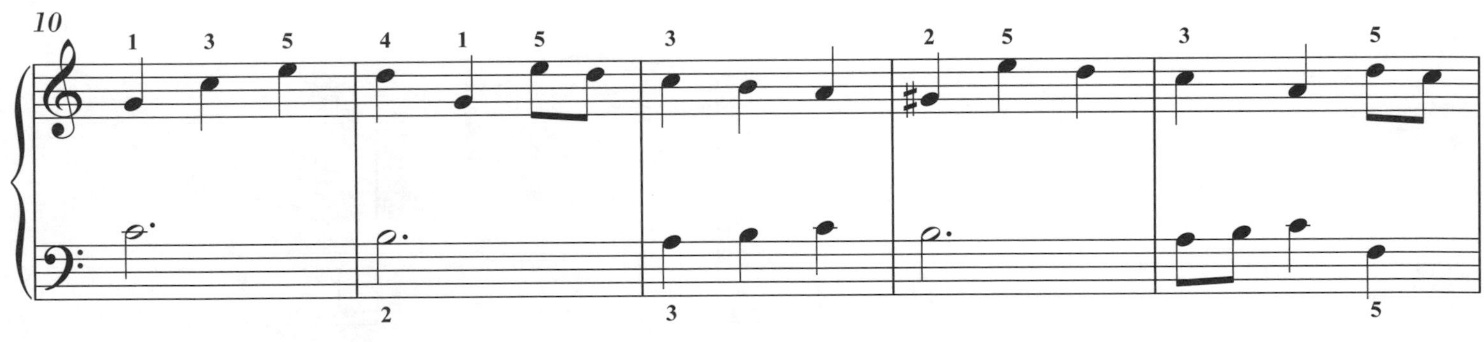

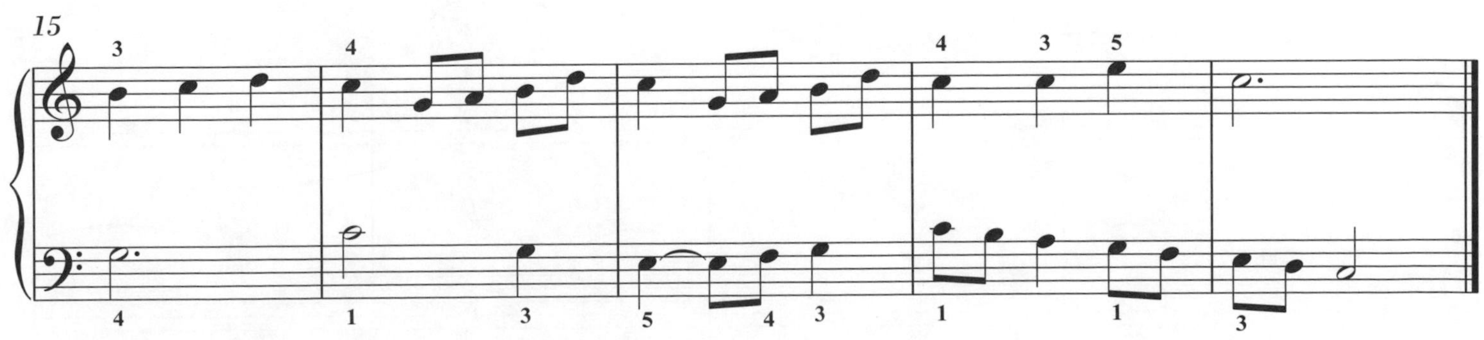

Madrigal

from *Album for the Very Young,* Op. 103

Mélanie Bonis

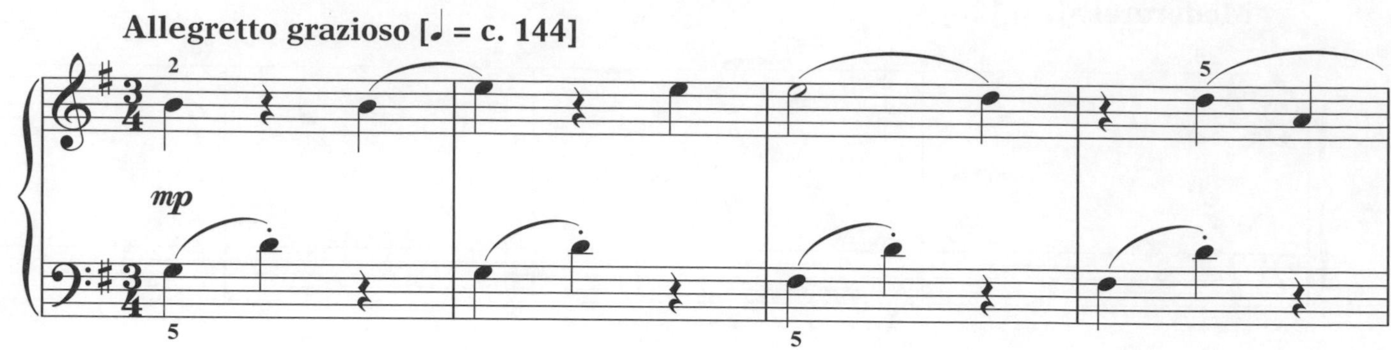

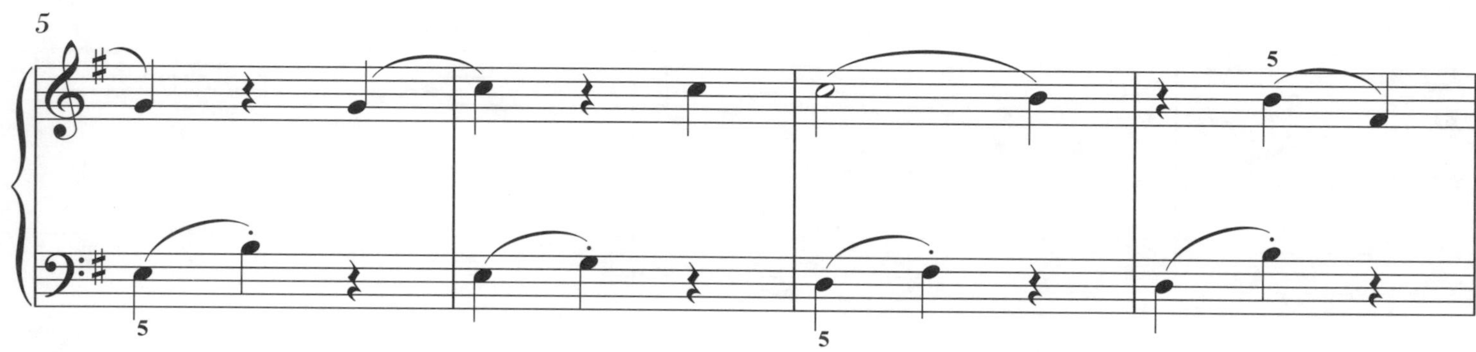

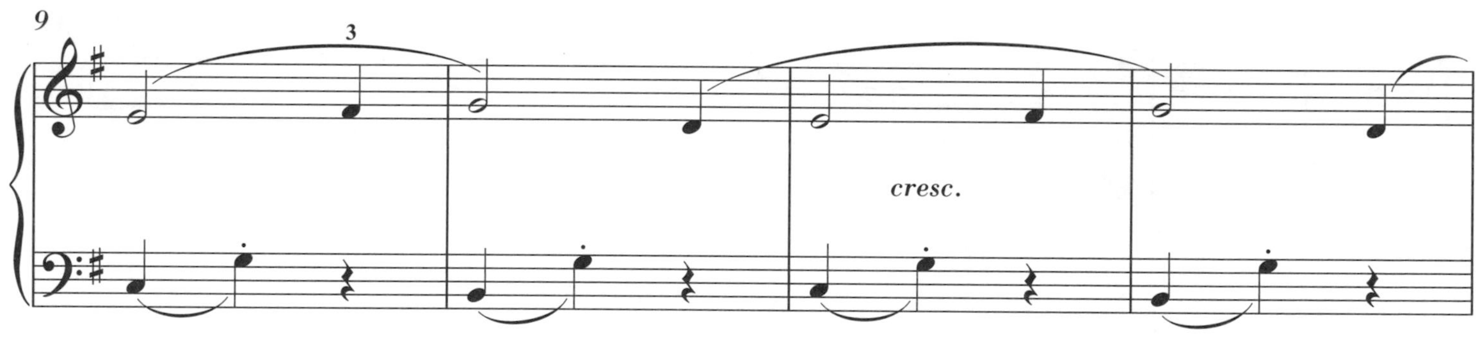

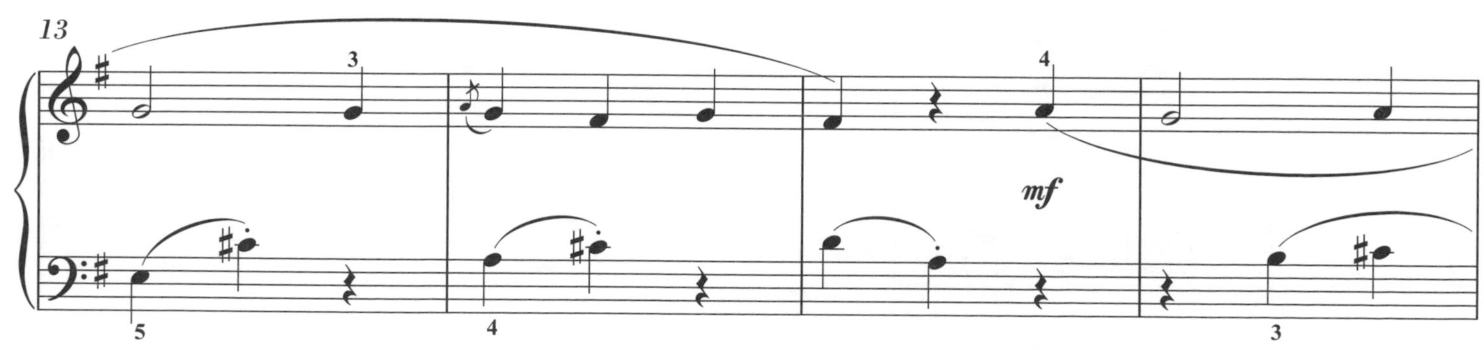

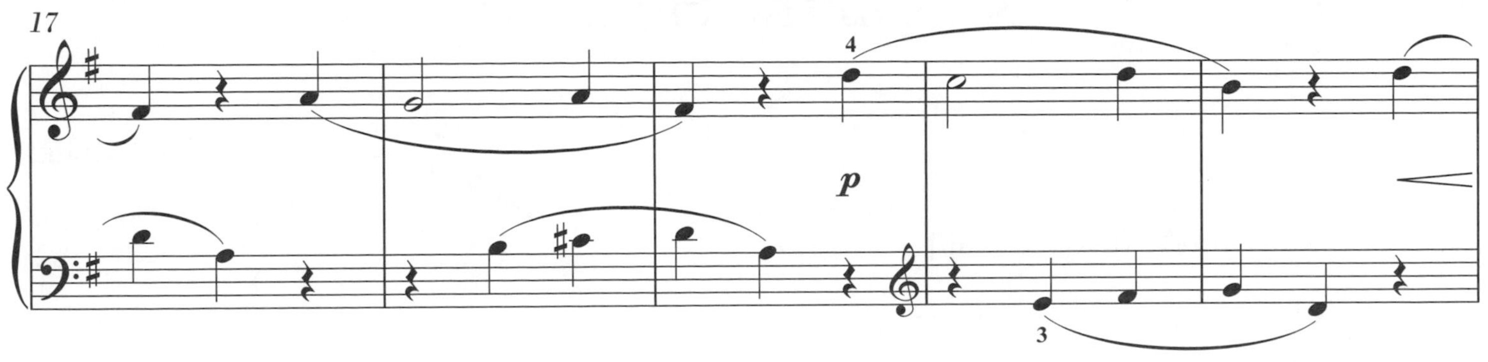
17
4
p
3

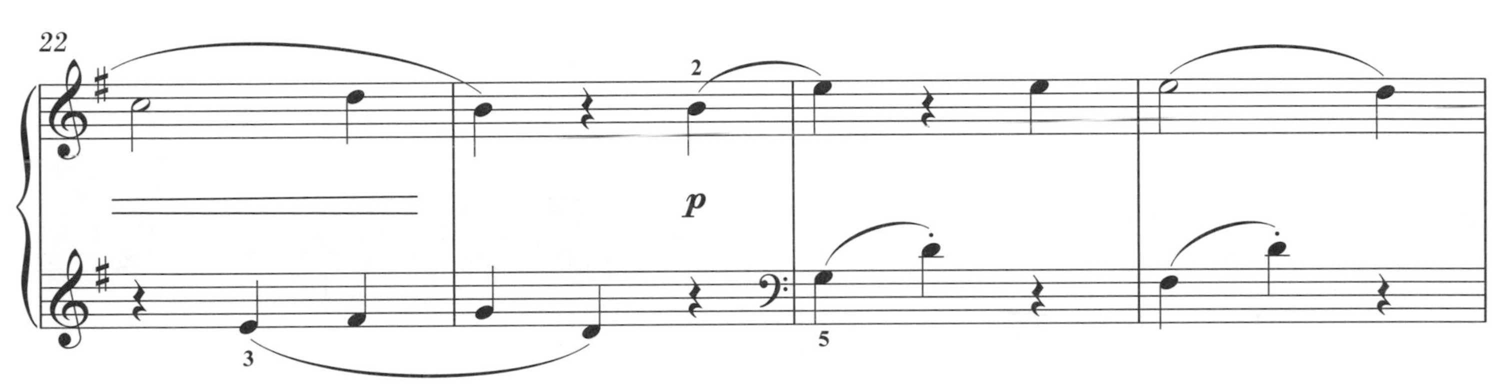
22
2
p
3
5

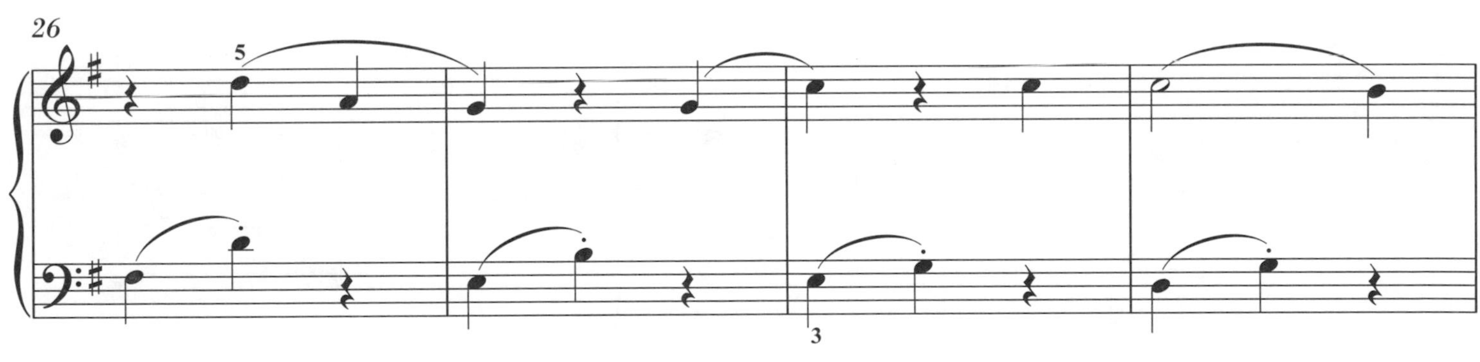
26
5
3

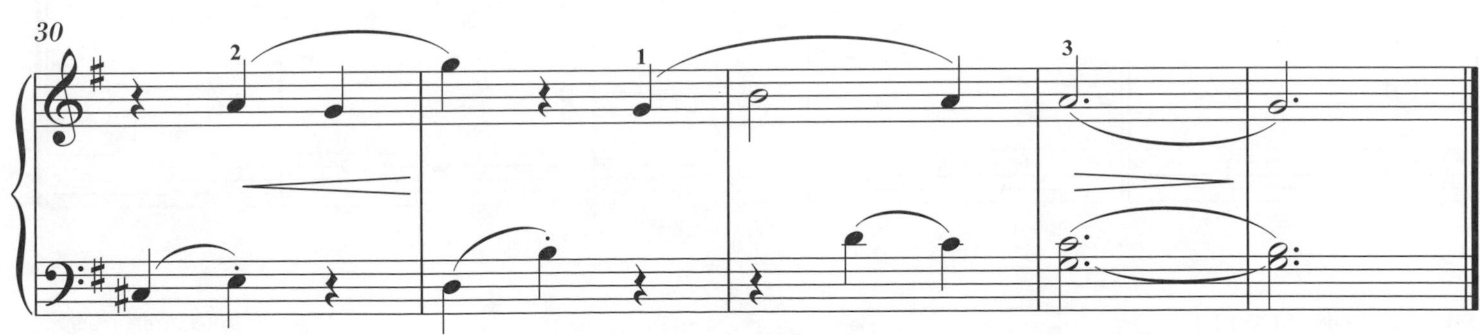
30
2
1
3

On the Hunt

Jean-Michel Arnaud

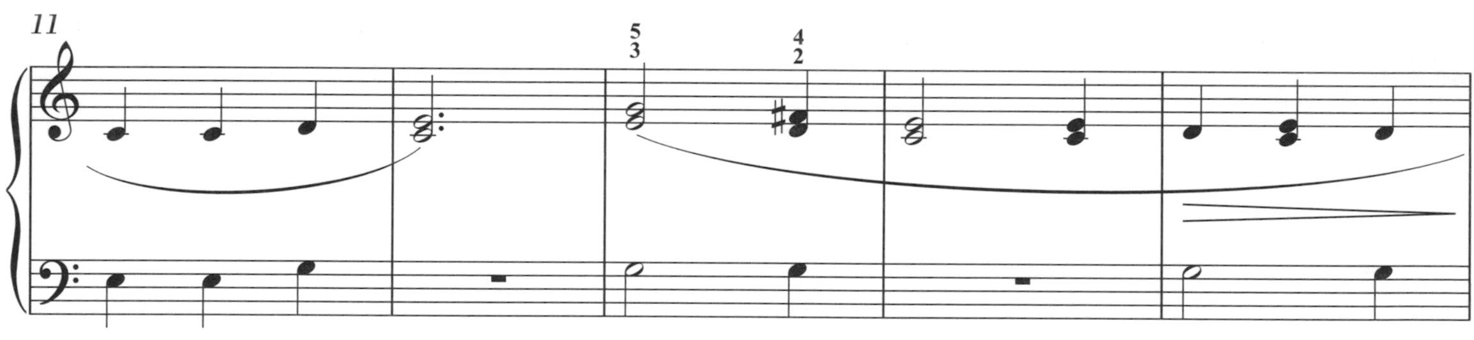

Blue Note

Olivier Hauray

The Injured Bird

Jean-Michel Arnaud

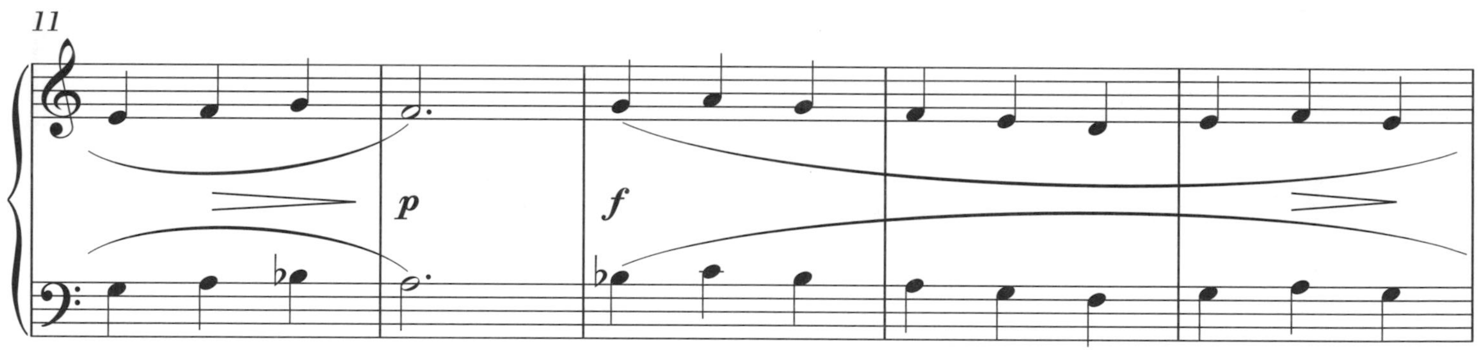

The Fortune Teller

Jean-Michel Arnaud